DISCARDED

Valentine's Day

Josie Keogh

PowerKiDS press

New York

Published in 2013 by The Rosen Publishing Group, Inc.
29 East 21st Street, New York, NY 10010

First Edition

Editor: Amelie von Zumbusch
Book Design: Andrew Povolny

Photo Credits: Cover, p. 9 KidStock/Blend Images/Getty Images; p. 5 Jupiter Images/Brand X Pictures/Thinkstock; pp. 7, 15, 21 iStockphoto/Thinkstock; p. 11 Digital Vision/Thinkstock; p. 13 Fuse/Getty Images; p. 17 LWA/Dann Tardif/Blend Images/Getty Images; p. 19 KidStock/Blend Images/Getty Images; p. 23 Fototeca Storica Nazionale/Photodisc/Getty Images.

Library of Congress Cataloging-in-Publication Data

Keogh, Josie.
  Valentine's day / by Josie Keogh. — 1st ed.
     p. cm. — (Powerkids readers: happy holidays!)
  Includes index.
  ISBN 978-1-4488-9627-1 (library binding) — ISBN 978-1-4488-9710-0 (pbk.) —
  ISBN 978-1-4488-9711-7 (6-pack)
  1. Valentine's Day—Juvenile literature. I. Title.
  GT4925.K46 2013
  394.2618—dc23
                              2012020632

Manufactured in the United States of America

CPSIA Compliance Information: Batch #W13PK3: For Further Information contact Rosen Publishing, New York, New York at 1-800-237-9932

Contents

It is Valentine's Day!

The day honors love.

Give a card.

8

Teachers get the most cards.

Give a gift.

13

Red **roses** stand for true love.

15

Eat a treat.

16

17

Chocolate is the top-selling candy.

Lovebirds are from Africa.

Cupid was the Roman
love god.

23

WORDS TO KNOW

chocolate

lovebirds

rose

INDEX

WEBSITES

Due to the changing nature of Internet links, PowerKids Press has developed an online list of websites related to the subject of this book. This site is updated regularly. Please use this link to access the list:
www.powerkidslinks.com/pkrhh/vday/

24